GREAT RULERS
OF THE
AFRICAN PAST

The aim of Zenith Books is to present the history of minority groups in the United States and their participation in the growth and development of the country. Through histories and biographies written by leading historians in collaboration with established writers for young people, Zenith Books will increase the awareness of minority group members of their own heritage and at the same time develop among all people an understanding and appreciation of that heritage.

Dr. JOHN HOPE FRANKLIN, Chairman of the History Department at the University of Chicago, has also taught at Brooklyn College, Fisk University, and Howard University. For the year 1962–63, he was William Pitt Professor of American History and Institutions at Cambridge University in England. He is the author of many books including *From Slavery to Freedom, The Militant South, Reconstruction after the Civil War,* and *The Emancipation Proclamation.*

SHELLEY UMANS is Director for the Center for Innovation for the Board of Education of the City of New York, a specialist in reading instruction and a member of the instructional staff of Teachers College, Columbia University. For more than ten years, she has been a consultant to many major urban school systems throughout the United States. She is the author of *New Trends in Reading Instruction* and *Designs for Reading Programs.*

LAVINIA DOBLER is Head Librarian at Scholastic Magazines. She has taught in her native Riverton, Wyoming, and in California and Puerto Rico. Among her numerous books and articles are *Customs and Holidays Around the World, Cyrus McCormick: Farmer Boy,* and *Arrow Book of the United Nations.*

WILLIAM A. BROWN is an historian who has specialized in the history of Africa. He is the recipient of a Foreign Area Fellowship which has taken him to Africa for further research and study.

DR. PHILIP CURTIN is Professor of History at the University of Wisconsin and head of the African Studies Program at the University. His latest book is *The Image of Africa.*

YVONNE JOHNSON is a designer and illustrator of books for young people. She did illustrations for the *Golden Treasury of Knowledge,* and is the designer for the *Crowell Collier 1964–65 Year Book.*

Other Outstanding Zenith Books

FOUR TOOK FREEDOM, by Philip Sterling and Rayford Logan. The lives of Harriet Tubman, Frederick Douglass, Robert Smalls, and Blanche K. Bruce.

A GLORIOUS AGE IN AFRICA, by Daniel Chu and Elliott Skinner. The story of three great African empires.

A GUIDE TO AFRICAN HISTORY, by Basil Davidson, revised and edited by Haskel Frankel. A general survey of the African past from earliest times to the present.

LIFT EVERY VOICE, by Dorothy Sterling and Benjamin Quarles. The lives of W. E. B. Du Bois, Mary Church Terrell, Booker T. Washington, and James Weldon Johnson.

PASSAGE TO THE GOLDEN GATE, by Daniel Chu and Samuel C. Chu. A history of the Chinese in America to 1910.

PIONEERS AND PATRIOTS, by Lavinia Dobler and Edgar A. Toppin. The lives of six Negroes of the colonial and revolutionary eras.

TIME OF TRIAL, TIME OF HOPE, by Milton Meltzer and August Meier. The history of the Negro in America from 1919 to 1941.

THE UNFINISHED MARCH, by Carol Drisko and Edgar A. Toppin. The Negro in the United States from Reconstruction to World War I.

WORTH FIGHTING FOR, by Agnes McCarthy and Lawrence Reddick. A history of the Negro in the United States during the Civil War and Reconstruction.

GREAT RULERS
OF THE
AFRICAN PAST

Lavinia Dobler and William A. Brown

SPECIAL CONSULTANT:

Philip Curtin, Ph.D.

ILLUSTRATED BY YVONNE JOHNSON

ZENITH BOOKS
DOUBLEDAY & COMPANY, INC., GARDEN CITY, NEW YORK

The Zenith Books edition, published simultaneously in hardbound and paperback volumes, is the first publication of *Great Rulers of the African Past*.

Zenith Books edition: 1965

CONTENTS

MANSA MUSA
Powerful Ruler of Mali
(1312–1337)

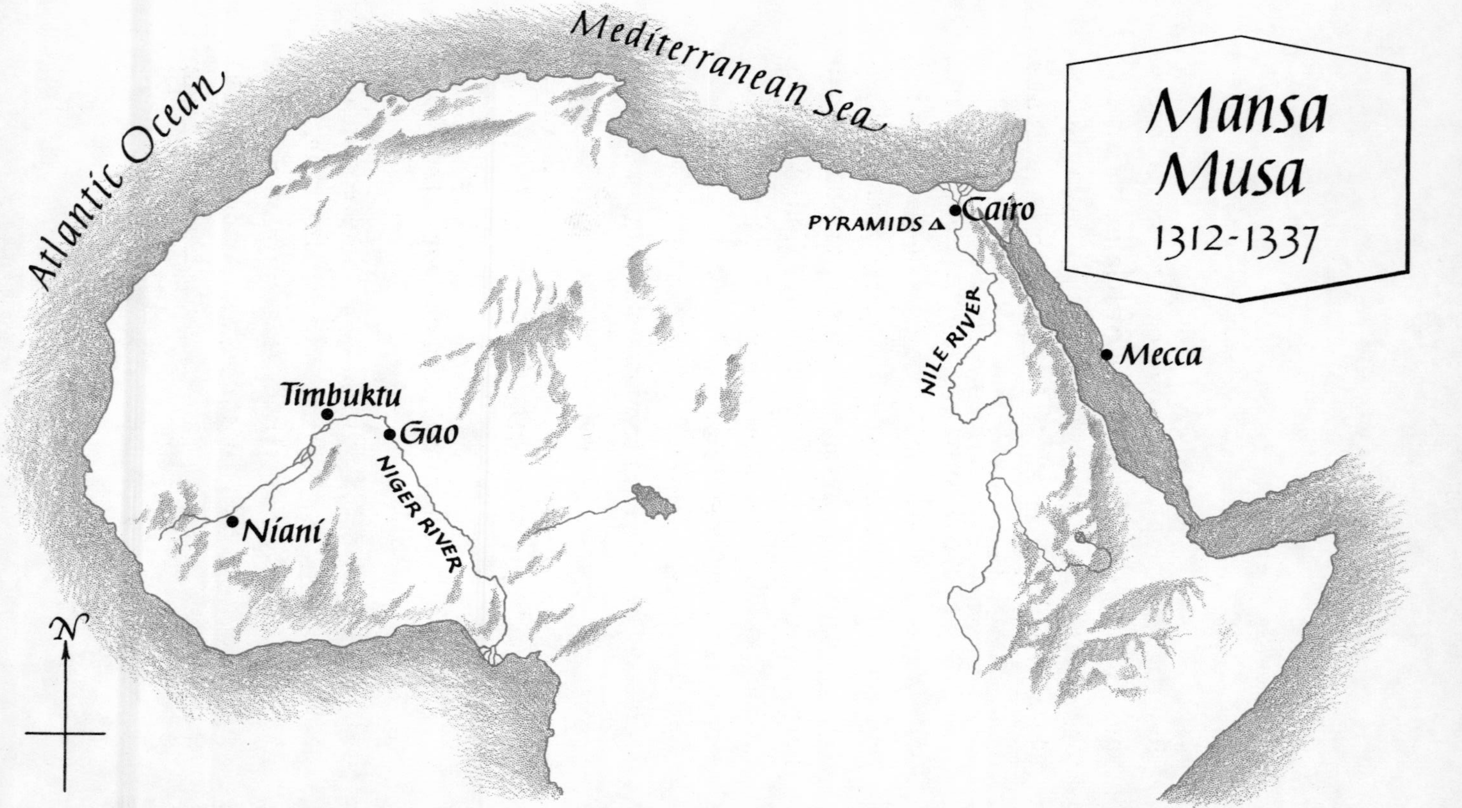

Mansa
Musa
1312-1337

Mecca

Cairo

PYRAMIDS △

NILE RIVER

Mediterranean Sea

Atlantic Ocean

Gao

Timbuktu

NIGER RIVER

Niani

N

The sun beat down fiercely on the royal courtyard. Shadows made strange patterns on the buildings of dried mud that were the king's headquarters. The gold and silver strips lining the high windows of these buildings sparkled.

A huge crowd waited eagerly in the courtyard. Some were traders from the north who had traveled hundreds of miles to reach this city, *Niani* (ni-ah-ni), the capital of Mali. Many loyal subjects of the king also waited. All of them were tired, but they did not mind. Soon Mansa Musa I, ruler of Mali, would come before them.

An Egyptian merchant turned to a trader from Morocco. "Is it true, as they say, that Mansa Musa is a generous and virtuous prince?"

The Moroccan nodded. "I have come to Mali often. Mansa Musa is indeed a good ruler and a devout Moslem."

"Has he believed in that religion long?" the Egyptian asked.

"He and his ancestors have been followers of Mohammed for perhaps three centuries," the other man replied. "Mansa Musa is descended from *Sundiata* (sun-di-ah-ta). The *Mandingoes* (man-din-goes) now consider Sundiata their national hero, but many

3

of the people of his own time did not like him." The Moroccan smiled. "But it is different with this king. Mansa Musa is loved by all his people."

"Are they all Moslems, too?" asked the Egyptian.

"The men who run the government are Moslems," the Moroccan explained. "But they are few compared to the many people who are still pagans. I understand this troubles Mansa Musa. Too many of his people worship many gods, including the sun, moon, and stars. He would like to have all his subjects worship the one God the Moslems call Allah."

The crowd waited respectfully to see Mansa Musa not only because he was a good man, but also because he was a powerful one.

When Musa became the *Mansa,* which means king or emperor, the kingdom of Mali covered thousands of miles in West Africa. It extended from the mouth of the *Senegal* (say-nay-gal) River on the Atlantic Ocean to the right bank of the Niger River. On the north, Mansa Musa's power went deep into the great Sahara Desert where he controlled salt deposits and copper mines. During his reign, Mansa Musa increased the size of his rich kingdom. At one time or another, from thirteen to twenty-four regions of Africa were loyal to him.

Suddenly the chattering of the crowd stopped. A door in the king's headquarters was opened by a court attendant. Musicians carrying gold and silver two-stringed guitars came into the courtyard.

Then came the king himself. He was a tall Negro, with black hair, a heavy beard, and pale gold skin. He held an arrow in his right hand and the quiver on his back was filled with gold-tipped arrows. Instead of a crown, he wore a turban of gold cloth. His short robe was deep red, made of fine cloth woven in Europe. His full trousers had been sewn from yards of elegant material.

In front of Mansa Musa walked singers who rang gold and silver bells. Many armed slaves and servants followed him. His ivory throne stood on a special platform in the courtyard. Before climbing the steps to the platform, Mansa Musa stopped and studied the people assembled in his honor. His face was calm and his deep black eyes shone with kindness. Then he walked up the silver steps to his throne, which was protected from the sun by a richly decorated awning of rare silk. His manner showed great pride and confidence.

Special visitors were now summoned by servants to speak to the king. This day Mansa Musa was eager to see a particular loyal subject. He had sent this man on a mission to the south. Mansa Musa hoped the peoples of the south would become Moslems. This would be a great accomplishment for his kingdom and for his faith.

Musicians announced Mansa Musa's entrance to the waiting crowd.

This man now came before him. He knelt, knocking his elbows hard against the ground. Then he stood up and reported respectfully. "Your Majesty, this is not the time to pursue the *Wangara* (wang-garah) people of the south. They have refused to accept our faith." He continued slowly. "The miners of Wangara even threatened to stop producing gold if they were forced to become Moslems." The man paused thoughtfully. "It would not be wise to try to force them. The Wangara are skilled at forest fighting. They use poisoned arrows. The tsetse fly that brings the deadly sleeping sickness could destroy our army."

Mansa Musa was disappointed. Yet, much of Mali's trade depended on the gold mined by the Wangara people. Also Mansa Musa had deep respect for the rights of all peoples. So he would follow the man's advice.

At this time in history, Mali was about the size of Western Europe. It controlled great wealth—gold, iron, copper, salt—and grew plentiful crops of food. There was also much learning. The scholars of Mali used the Arabic language, just as scholars in every country in Europe used the Latin language.

Mansa Musa's subjects were hard-working people. Many villages had craftsmen: woodcarvers, silver-

The people of Mali ate wild buffalo, elephants, and crocodiles, which they hunted with poisoned arrows and spears.

smiths, goldsmiths, coppersmiths, weavers, tanners, and dyers.

But of greatest importance to the kingdom of Mali was its political organization. The government Mansa

9

Musa led was a strong one. It was able to keep all parts of the kingdom united.

Mansa Musa had a large army of which he was justly proud. There were about 100,000 men in this army, including 10,000 cavalrymen. They used some camels, but preferred Arabian horses. The officers, soldiers, and personal guard of the king had control over particular regions of his territory. They may have been paid by these regions. Mansa Musa also gave them gifts of gold, clothing, and horses.

Giving clothes as a gift seemed to be a Malian custom. Every time a horseman performed an outstanding deed, the king dressed him in wide trousers. For additional acts of valor, the horseman's trousers were made a little bit wider. The trousers were wide in the seat and narrow in the legs. This kind of trousers is used today among the Moslems of the Sudan.

The Moslem people of Mali were deeply religious. Every Friday, the Moslem holy day, all of them went to the mosque, which is the Moslem house of worship. Many officials sent their servants to the mosque early to save places for them. The Mansa would come to the service on horseback. With him would be the chief judge, the scholars and the *imam* (ee-mam), or prayer leader.

When Mansa Musa had ruled for more than ten years, he still had not made his pilgrimage to Mecca.

Because he was a good Moslem, he was very troubled about this.

The journey to the holy city of Mecca is one of the five duties of a devout Moslem. At least once in their lifetime, all Moslems who are healthy and can afford it, are expected to go to Mecca. The other four duties include special prayers, times for fasting, and alms-giving. These are done wherever the Moslem lives.

Mansa Musa talked to his council about going on a pilgrimage to Mecca. The members all agreed that he should plan to go as soon as possible.

Many months of preparations were necessary for this great trip. Mansa Musa sent messengers to all parts of his kingdom to request food and money.

It was no hardship for the people to supply great quantities of food. The people of Mali grew most of their own food. Native produce included sorghum, rice, yams, beans, and onions. These they contributed to their ruler.

From the baobab tree they got medicinal liquids, red dye, and a kind of white meal for bread. The shea-butter tree, like the baobab tree, was found in many parts of Mali. Its fruit looked like a lemon and tasted like a pear. From the kernel of this fruit the people made an oil which they used to make soap and used as fuel for lamps.

Cotton was grown in most parts of Mali. It was

made into cloth. The people in the religious caravan would be gone for a long time, so extra clothes had to be made.

Gold was the most important item Mansa Musa would need for his long trip. He got the gold he needed by trading with the Wangara people. For their gold Mansa Musa sent them copper bars from the mines of the Sahara, along with salt bars, grains, cowrie shells, which were used as money, livestock, and cloth.

In the year 1324, the twelfth year of Mansa Musa's reign, the caravan set out from *Timbuktu* (tim-buck-too).

Never had the people of West Africa seen such a sight. The caravan started northeast through the desert under a cloudless blue sky. There were thousands of people and hundreds of camels. It was a magnificent parade. It seemed to stretch for miles. There were long columns of gayly decorated camels carrying Mansa Musa's officials and others from the court. There were camels loaded with chests full of gifts and golds, hundreds of servants. Some say there were 8000 in the group, some say 60,000!

Among the richly dressed people who went with Mansa Musa and his wife were many Moslem leaders and wise men. Important chiefs had been chosen to go also. This was a special honor in recognition of their services to Mansa Musa. However, he had also chosen them for another reason. He wanted to be sure they would not plot against his son, who would rule Mali while he was away.

The journey across the Sahara Desert was long and exhausting. Mansa Musa did not know it at the time, but the Sahara is the world's largest desert region. Probably his caravan was able to travel about thirty miles a day and it was several thousand miles to Mecca!

There were days when they saw nothing but miles and miles of endless sand dunes. Some of these wind-blown hills of sand were only a few feet high; some were several hundred feet high.

Arriving at an oasis—a place in the desert where grass and trees grow and water can be found—would put everyone in good spirits. After sunset when it was not so hot, they would see gazelles, hares, and jackals at the water hole. But during the day there were few animals to watch. Only the desert fly was always with them, to bite and annoy them.

The camels did not seem to mind the flies. Goose-necked and hump-backed, these beasts are among the ugliest and meanest of creatures. However shaggy, awkward-looking, and stiff-legged, these great bur-den-bearers are exactly right for desert travel. Camels have overhanging eyelids and long lashes, which protect their eyes from sun and sand. They can close their nostrils tight against the driving sand of desert storms. Without these "ships of the desert," as they are often called, Mansa Musa's caravan would not have been able to make this long, long journey.

The pilgrims arrived in Egypt on the night of a lunar eclipse in May 1324. They stopped at the foot of the pyramids.

When the Sultan of Egypt learned of their arrival, he immediately sent his representative to the Mansa. The King of Mali greeted the sultan's representative with great politeness. But, even though Mansa Musa spoke fluent Arabic, he would talk to the Egyptian only through an interpreter. In this way he showed his independence as a powerful ruler equal to the Sultan of Egypt.

The representative extended cordial greetings in the name of the sultan. He said that the sultan would like Mansa Musa and his royal family to come to the palace in Cairo to meet him.

Mansa Musa shook his head. He said, "I come in order to make the Hajj, the holy pilgrimage to Mecca, not for any other purpose. I do not wish to mix my Hajj with anything else."

The sultan's representative tried to persuade the King of Mali to reconsider. He explained how honored the sultan would be. However, the Egyptian realized why Mansa Musa was not eager to come. The king from Mali knew he would have to kiss the ground before the sultan or else kiss his hand. That was the custom in Egypt. Yet Mansa Musa was a king in his own right. He did not want to perform such an act of submission.

Finally he accepted the invitation. He entered Cairo in July 1324.

When he appeared in the sultan's presence, Mansa Musa was asked to kiss the ground. He refused.

Instead, he turned to the sultan and with royal dignity he said, "I will prostrate myself only before God." Saying this, he knelt and kissed the ground —to honor Allah, not the sultan. After this ceremony, he stood up and with kingly grace walked toward the sultan.

The sultan was instantly impressed by this richly dressed ruler with the bearing of an aristocrat. He had not expected to see such a strong-looking man.

The sultan rose from his throne to greet his distinguished visitor. He invited Mansa Musa to sit next to him as a sign of respect. They talked for a long time. The ruler of Egypt was eager to learn more about this fabulous kingdom south and west of his own.

Before Mansa Musa left the palace, the sultan presented many gifts to his new friend. These gifts included rich garments for the king and horses with carved saddles and bridles.

Mansa Musa was overcome with such a display of wealth and splendor. "As ruler of Mali, I thank you," he told his host.

There were other gifts almost as impressive and beautiful for his officers.

The sultan also provided camels to carry the special presents, as well as others for the people to ride. They were also equipped with carved saddles. The sultan gave orders that Mansa Musa's caravan must be well provided with food and other provisions. Stations to feed the animals were set up along the route. He also sent word that all of his local governors were to show the ruler of Mali great respect.

Mansa Musa was overwhelmed with the sultan's thoughtfulness. Again he thanked him.

The sultan smiled graciously. "You still have miles to go before you reach your destination," he said. "My trusted guide will go with you so you will not get lost on the way."

The guide was pleased to have this task. He considered it a great honor. He reported later that he and the others in the caravan wore magnificent clothes. He was impressed with Mansa Musa's consideration for the poor. He admired Mansa Musa and spoke of him as a "great man" with "greatness of soul."

Mansa Musa had enjoyed the attention he received in Cairo, but he was now more eager than ever to reach Mecca. At one point, a wide channel of a branch of the Nile River delayed them for a number of days. All the people, the camels, and all the baggage had to be loaded on boats and taken across the water.

Finally they reached the holy land! Mansa Musa saw for the first time the sacred city that is so important to Moslems. Mecca lies in a narrow sandy valley between hills that rise from Arabia's Red Sea coast. The winding streets of the city were lined with tall stone houses with shuttered balconies.

Then he saw the Great Mosque!

The Great Mosque in Mecca was—and still is—the center of worship for Moslems from all over the world. It has many arches which are supported by pillars, with tall minarets, or towers, at the corners of the long arcade. A small flat-roofed stone building called the *Kaaba* (kah-ba) is in the courtyard of the Great Mosque. It contains the famous black stone. The archangel Gabriel is supposed to have given this stone to Abraham.

Mansa Musa as a devout Moslem began the ceremonies of the pilgrimage almost as soon as he entered the sacred city. He had already shaved his head and put on special clothes. His wife wore a loose cloak and veil.

Mansa Musa had his head shaved in preparation for the ceremonies of his pilgrimage.

At the Great Mosque he recited the prayers. He kissed the holy black stone of the Kaaba. Then he circled the building seven times, three times running and four times walking. He drank from the sacred well of Zem-Zem and he hurried seven times between the hills called *Safa* (sah-fa) and *Marwah*.

These ceremonies are based on ancient religious traditions that Mansa Musa knew well. According to religious legend, Ishmael, son of Abraham, the old Testament patriarch, had almost died in the desert. Then the angel Gabriel showed Ishmael's mother,

Hagar, the Zem-Zem well. The "running" from Safa to Marwah relives for the pilgrim Hagar's frantic search for water. Abraham is believed to have built the first Kaaba after Gabriel brought him the black stone from Heaven.

On the ninth day of the ceremony, Mansa Musa journeyed to Mount *Arafat* (á-ra-fat) where he took his stand at noon and recited prayers until sunset. On his return from the mountain, Mansa Musa threw stones at three pillars that represent devils. He went through the ceremony of sacrificing an animal. He gave the meat to the poor people in Mecca. After that service, Mansa Musa's head was again shaved. He put on his full trousers and flowing robes. He now had the coveted title of Hajji, for he had made the Hajj, or pilgrimage. Proudly he wore the special turban of the Hajji.

While in Arabia, Mansa Musa met a Spanish Arab from the city of Granada. This man, *Es-Saheli* (es-sa-he-li); was deeply religious and very wise. Besides being a poet, he was also an architect. The king liked him immediately. Here was a scholar who would be able to help him in Mali, Mansa Musa decided.

The two men often talked together. One day Mansa Musa said, "I would like you to return to Mali with me. We need men with your talents."

The architect smiled, but he didn't say anything

19

for a few minutes. Then he replied to the king, whom he had come to admire, "Your majesty, I shall be honored to return with you and to help in any way I am able."

Mansa Musa stayed a long time in Mecca. He seemed in no hurry to start back to Africa.

"I am getting old," he told one of his loyal subjects. "When I return home, I will turn over my kingdom to my son. Then I shall come back here to remain in this holiest of cities."

But Mansa Musa never returned to Mecca.

On his return trip, Mansa Musa again stopped in Cairo. It was January 1325. Again he received honors and gifts. Mansa Musa in turn presented beautiful articles to the Egyptians. These were both things he had purchased in the holy land and gifts of gold.

He had left Mali with many loads of gold which he spent during his pilgrimage. Some he gave to the tribes which he had passed on his way from Mali to Cairo; some in Cairo; some between Cairo and Arabia. When he was ready to leave Cairo he had to borrow some money for the remainder of his trip.

Mansa Musa had been so generous in Cairo that he had no trouble borrowing from the leading merchants. After he returned home, he seems to have paid back all of his debts. Some of the lenders went with him to Mali. Others sent collectors and representatives.

The caravan returned in triumph to Mali. Never before had the people had such a happy occasion to celebrate. They were filled with joy and pride at the accomplishment of their emperor.

He had been gone for a long time. They had had some word from traders and merchants about the caravan. But now that he had returned safely, they could really rejoice. Special services were celebrated

Everyone rejoiced at Mansa Musa's safe return from Mecca.

in the mosque. There were so many people who wanted to attend that hundreds had to stand outside.

And there were feasts for days.

Shortly after Mansa Musa returned, Es-Saheli built an auditorium in the capital city, using Spanish and North African architecture. The building was square with a cupola. It was coated with plaster and decorated with intricate carving. Mansa Musa was pleased, because he realized it was far stronger than other buildings in the city.

"This is a great monument and will still be standing long after we are gone," he told the architect, giving him a generous gift of gold.

The king had a royal residence built for himself in Timbuktu and also a mosque in the city of *Gao* (ga-ow). Probably both were planned by Es-Saheli.

Mansa Musa was a great and strong ruler. His pilgrimage to Mecca spread his fame through Egypt and Arabia, across the Mediterranean Sea to Europe. Foreign merchants came to Mali and settled there, increasing trade with all parts of North Africa.

Until his death in 1337, Mansa Musa continued improving his empire. He had always encouraged trade. His strong army helped very much in achieving this aim. It protected the land and the people who traveled through it.

Moslem scholars and judges were respected people

in Mali. The many beautiful buildings built by the Arab architect also helped to make Mali a great center of culture in West Africa.

Until the nineteenth century, Europeans continued to think of Mansa Musa's empire as an Eldorado, a fabulous land of gold.

SUNNI ALI BER
The Conqueror
(1464–1492)

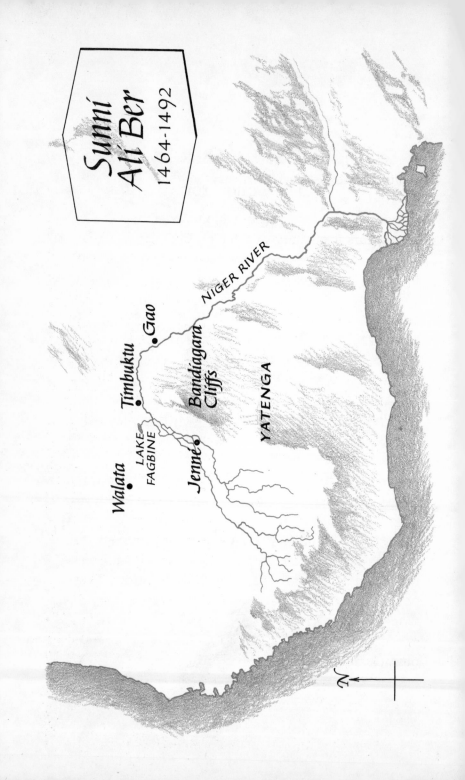

A messenger ran swiftly toward the city of Gao, capital of the West African *Songhay* (song-gay) kingdom.

Two guards stood at the wide wooden gates. They held spears in readiness to defend the entrance. They stopped the stranger, whose face was covered with the yellow dust of the desert.

The young man bowed low. "I have an important message for your king, *Sunni Ali Ber* (soon-ni ah-lee beer)." He was exhausted from running the long distance from Timbuktu to Gao. "I have instructions under penalty of death to deliver it only to your sultan himself."

"Who sent you?" one of the guards demanded.

"My master," the messenger replied, lowering his voice, "the Governor of Timbuktu."

The two guards approached and searched him. When they were sure he had no concealed knives, they beckoned to the soldiers inside the gate.

Escorted by more than a dozen armed men, the stranger from Timbuktu was taken through the narrow, winding streets to the king's headquarters. There he waited for the great Sunni Ali to receive him. Although the ruler had many secretaries, counselors, treasurers, and captains, he handled all important business himself.

The messenger was escorted by soldiers through the narrow streets to the king's headquarters.

Pages stood on the silk carpet behind the throne, holding shields and gold-hilted swords. Other attendants, in a row straight as palm trees, were near the platform. All waited for their leader and ruler.

At last the royal musicians sounded a roll on the drums and Sunni Ali made his grand entrance.

He was called "Sunni" which in Songhay means successor or replacement of the ruler, rather than king. This title had become the tradition over 150 years before. In Songhay *Ber* means "great." So the ruler's name, Ali Ber, meant Ali the Great.

Tall and strong, he commanded the respect of everyone. On his black hair was a gold turban and his dark brown skin shone like satin. His long flowing robe and full trousers of gold cloth sparkled in the bright sunlight. He walked proudly to his ivory throne, seating himself under a canopy that protected him from the intense sun.

One of Sunni Ali's royal counselors approached him and spoke. Sunni Ali nodded.

Accompanied by soldiers, the man from Timbuktu walked slowly toward the king. The counselor turned to the stranger.

"You have a secret message for our emperor?" he asked. The man nodded. "I will deliver it to him." The counselor held out his hand.

The messenger hesitated. Then, he handed the

tiny scroll to the king's servant. The royal officer in turn handed the scroll to the emperor.

Sunni Ali scowled as he unrolled the parchment. His expression changed as he read the message.

"I must answer *Ammar* (am-mar) in Timbuktu right away," he said.

The scribe came with parchment and quill. Sunni Ali rapidly dictated his reply to Ammar.

Then he turned to his counselor. "Tell the messenger to return in haste to Timbuktu. Ammar is waiting impatiently for my answer." Sunni Ali looked very pleased indeed.

Sunni Ali Ber had waited more than four years for the opportunity which this secret message gave him—the opportunity to capture Timbuktu. This great city of merchants and scholars had never belonged to the Songhay rulers. Now its governor had asked for Sunni Ali's help.

Sunni Ali Ber, like Mansa Musa of Mali, had established a central government in the Songhay kingdom. By means of taxes and trade, he gained wealth and power that amazed people in the fifteenth century. Today his record is just as impressive.

The leaders who had ruled the lands in West Africa before him had built a strong foundation. Sunni Ali was ambitious. He added more territory and made his empire even stronger. The Songhay country was important because it was on the Niger River. Its flat plains extended to the great forest on the south and to the great desert on the north. On the east the Songhay land was bounded by the *Hombori* (hahm-boar-ee) plateau, and a long, high, steep face of rock known as the *Bandiagara* (ban-dee-ah-gah-rah).

What motive inspired Sunni Ali to further conquests? We can never really know. He was quick thinking and daring and seemed to have no fear. He was determined only to conquer.

Sunni Ali was probably not a pagan. He did accept the pagan traditions of many of the Songhay people. When he came to power he was given as emblems of his authority a seal, a sword, and a Koran, the Moslem book of holy writings. Since most of the Songhay people were Moslems, it was traditional that the ruler also be a Moslem.

Yet he tolerated the traditional religion also. In his position as emperor he was outwardly a Moslem. He fasted during the holy month of Ramadan and gave alms to the mosques. As a descendant of pagan priests and magicians, he worshiped certain stones and trees. He made sacrifices to them. He consulted them when important decisions had to be made.

Sunni Ali Ber was as cunning in his governing council as he was on the battlefield. He played off

The royal counselor handed the scroll to Sunni Ali.

one enemy against another. His aim was a strong central power where he alone should dominate.

Now he turned his attention to Timbuktu. "It wasn't too long ago," he remarked to his trusted adviser, "that Ammar boasted to me that Timbuktu could repulse any assault. Remember that proud letter he sent me then?" Sunni Ali laughed aloud, thinking of Ammar's desperation.

For some years Timbuktu had been under the control of *Akil* (ah-keel), who lived in the desert, ruling a tribe of nomads. His governor in Timbuktu was Ammar.

Ammar, and before him, his father, collected the revenue—gold and food products. The understanding was that Ammar could keep one-third of the amount he collected. The rest went to Akil.

But recently Akil needed more money. So he had been raiding Timbuktu, taking even the third of the revenue that belonged to Ammar. Akil needed this money to take care of his warriors.

Ammar, of course, was furious. However, he was helpless unless he could get aid from another ruler. Sunni Ali Ber was powerful, he knew, and ruthless and ambitious. Just the right man to take care of Akil.

As Sunni Ali's army assembled, there was great excitement. They, too, had waited a long time to march against Timbuktu. Spears and other weapons flashed brightly in the sun. The men shouted joyfully to each other.

Ali Ber had given up the old type army in which all able men were called to fight. This resulted in crops left unplanted and neglected herds. He wanted a strong army, but not at the price of having his people go hungry.

So he had instructed his captains: "Pick strong men, but do not take everyone. Release those who are good farmers, herdsmen, and traders. It is wiser to have a smaller, well-trained permanent army than a big army of men who cannot handle weapons."

This strong force, composed of noble cavalrymen, nomad camel drivers and captive foot soldiers, lived in special camps. These men were trained for war. The horsemen were equipped with sabers, lances, javelins, and breastplates. The foot soldiers had bows and poisoned arrows.

Sunni Ali Ber rode into battle at the head of the cavalry. The king's flag waved high above, fluttering against the cloudless blue sky. The gold ornaments on the horses' bridles shone.

"To Timbuktu!" the emperor shouted.

"To Timbuktu!" the soldiers chorused, and the glorious words echoed for miles.

The army moved north along the Niger River. It

At the head of the cavalry, Sunni Ali led his army to Timbuktu.

was a long, hot journey. Timbuktu was hundreds of miles away. But the soldiers and cavalrymen were in high spirits, eager for battle.

When Sunni Ali arrived at the outskirts of Timbuktu, Akil and his treacherous governor, Ammar, were standing on one of the highest sand dunes in the area. They watched the thousands of soldiers moving toward them.

"Where did Sunni Ali get so many warriors?" Akil asked.

Ammar, too, was amazed and disturbed. He had not known that the ruler from Gao had such a big army.

"Still they come!" Akil cried. "We cannot save Timbuktu. We are lost!" Akil looked suspiciously at his governor.

"What about our people in Timbuktu?" Ammar asked.

"You are the governor, not I," Akil said scornfully. And leaving his responsibility for the city, he fled immediately.

The people quickly learned that Akil had abandoned their city when he saw the strength of Sunni Ali's army. They too were filled with fear. Would their governor desert them? Many people packed a few possessions and left as quickly as possible.

Ammar gave orders to rush canoes to the Niger River to help Sunni Ali and his warriors cross the river. But when Ammar saw the Emperor of Gao set foot on the shore, he panicked. Now that he was saved, he regretted asking for this man's help. Ammar was afraid that Sunni Ali would seek revenge for the boasting letter he had sent two years before. Perhaps Sunni Ali would make him a prisoner or kill him.

Ammar hurried to his brother and persuaded him to stay and surrender the city in Ammar's place. The governor himself hastily left the city.

Sunni Ali Ber marched into Timbuktu and plundered the city. He was particularly cruel to the Moslem scholars. He feared their influence and power. Although he professed to be a Moslem, this made no difference.

Frightened by Sunni Ali's cruelty, everyone who could fled the city. This angered Sunni Ali so much that he massacred more people and chased and killed many who were trying to flee.

Because of the conquests of Sunni Ali, Arab merchants from the north who had been trading with other cities, now began to visit the markets of Timbuktu and Gao.

But Sunni Ali was not satisfied. He was obsessed with a great desire to conquer *Jenne* (jen).

"Jenne has never been conquered," the elder counselor reminded him. "Its brave people have successfully withstood a hundred assaults by the Kings of Mali."

Sunni Ali Ber glared at him. "They don't know my strength." He did not realize that the siege might take years.

Jenne was in the heart of the fertile region of rivers, lakes and swamps. It was one of the principal market cities of Africa. Here merchants traded salt from the north for the gold of the south.

Timbuktu and Jenne were rivals both in culture and in trade. But Jenne had many advantages over Timbuktu. Timbuktu had no natural defenses. Jenne was surrounded by a network of waterways which made it easy for traders to reach. These same waterways gave Jenne protection from invaders.

In Timbuktu, trade and learning were constantly interrupted by desert politics. But in Jenne, trade and learning were deeply rooted. Most of the scholars of Jenne were Negroes. Those of Timbuktu were mostly of Berber descent.

For seven long years Sunni Ali attacked Jenne. His army changed positions according to the seasons. The rise and fall of the waters around Jenne made the siege difficult. During the dry season, the soldiers camped just outside the city. When the river rose and the waters surrounded Jenne on all sides, they moved to a high hill.

Each year Sunni Ali expected to capture Jenne. The people resisted. This strengthened his determination, but his soldiers became discouraged.

However, even Sunni Ali began to think they might never take the city. But just before he was ready to give up the siege, he received news that made him continue. Word reached him that the people of Jenne were starving. It would not be long now.

The people of Jenne were desperate. The council of nobles knew of the suffering of the city. They also knew how cruel Sunni Ali Ber had been to the Moslem merchants and scholars in Timbuktu. Reluctantly they agreed to deliver Jenne to the conqueror from Gao.

The King of Jenne mounted his horse and rode to Sunni Ali's camp. He dismounted and approached the emperor to pay respect. Sunni Ali welcomed him with great ceremony. He was amazed that the King of Jenne was so young.

The king bowed. "I am but newly come to the throne, great Sunni Ali. My father died recently."

Sunni Ali ordered the young man to sit next to him. The king had not expected such good treatment from this ruthless conqueror, but he obeyed. From that time on, the chiefs of Jenne had the privilege of sitting on the same mat with the emperors of Gao and being treated as equals.

Sunni Ali Ber entered Jenne in triumph. Strangely, he did not loot the city or persecute the Moslems there. Perhaps he used different methods because these people were not friends of the hated nomads. He was as merciful to Jenne as he had been harsh to Timbuktu. The year was 1473.

Sunni Ali was especially pleased by the poise and beauty of the young king's mother. In a short time the conqueror of Jenne and the widowed queen were married.

But Sunni Ali did not remain long in Jenne. There were problems in the north. He was impatient to enlarge his empire. From that time on, Sunni Ali was almost constantly at war to bring the lands between Timbuktu and Jenne under his control.

Sunni Ali still hated the nomads who had once controlled Timbuktu. He had planned for a long time to take revenge on Akil and the rest who had fled. Akil and his followers had gone to Walata.

He thought for a long time about how to destroy Akil and add Walata to his empire. He knew it could not be done with his usual tactics. Something new would have to be done. Suddenly a plan came to him that seemed fantastic.

Ali Ber unrolled a parchment map and studied it. Lake *Fagbine* (fag-bee-nay) was nearly two hundred miles from Walata. Why not dig a canal from Lake

Sunni Ali was especially pleased by the poise and beauty of the widowed queen.

Fagbine to Walata? His soldiers could sail on the canal in their canoes. It would be an almost sure way to capture the city.

Sunni Ali called a council of his advisers. When

he told them his plan, they were speechless. Only their leader would ever have such a fantastic idea. It was impossible. They shook their heads.

"Nothing is impossible for Sunni Ali Ber!" the emperor shouted.

Soon hundreds of men began to dig under the hot sun. The emperor himself acted as supervisor. The canal was uppermost in his thoughts and he wanted to have it finished as soon as possible. He was busy overseeing the workmen, when a messenger arrived.

"They cannot do this!" Sunni Ali roared when he read the message. It said that the Mossi army, enemies of Sunni Ali, was on its way to attack his forces from the rear.

The emperor immediately had his men stop work on the canal. He never called them back to it.

He assembled his troops and led them into battle against the Mossi. This was in 1483.

Ali Ber conquered. He pursued the Mossi army south into their native *Yatenga* (yah-ting-ga). On his way back from Yatenga, he attacked the *Tombo* (tom-bow) people on the Bandiagara cliffs. This proved to be one of the few times Ali Ber was defeated. He was not only furious but humiliated.

"I shall get even!" Sunni Ali screamed at his army. "No one can do this to me. The Moslems are to blame!"

Sunni Ali himself supervised the digging of the canal.

Immediately, he headed toward Timbuktu and once again punished the Moslems. Afterward, he marched along the right bank of the Niger River, campaigning against the nomads who had been threatening the settled peoples.

Then Sunni Ali Ber disappeared!

There is complete mystery about his sudden end. The story is that he drowned in a small stream while attempting to cross it in a canoe. But all that is known for sure is that, in 1492, Ali Ber vanished, never to be seen again.

Although known to history as a tyrant and villain, today Sunni Ali Ber is recognized as a ruler of great historical importance. He was the first strong king to unite the Songhay people in this Sudan region. His Songhay kingdom eventually included thousands of square miles of land. This territory is now part of three West African countries—Mali, Niger, and Upper Volta.

It was Sunni Ali who divided the Songhay into provinces. He placed each under the control of one of his principal officers.

He used the Niger River as a highway for military transportation and trade. He understood the value of this waterway.

He promoted prosperity among his own people.

He first used professional soldiers and formed a permanent army.

He undertook water projects along the Niger, building dikes and canals.

The soldiers and many of the Songhay people of his time so admired him that they called him "most high," implying that he was like a god.

The twenty-eight years of the reign of Sunni Ali Ber—the great conqueror, engineer, and organizer—represents the highest point of Songhay civilization.

ASKIA MUHAMMAD
The Faithful Moslem
(1493–1528)

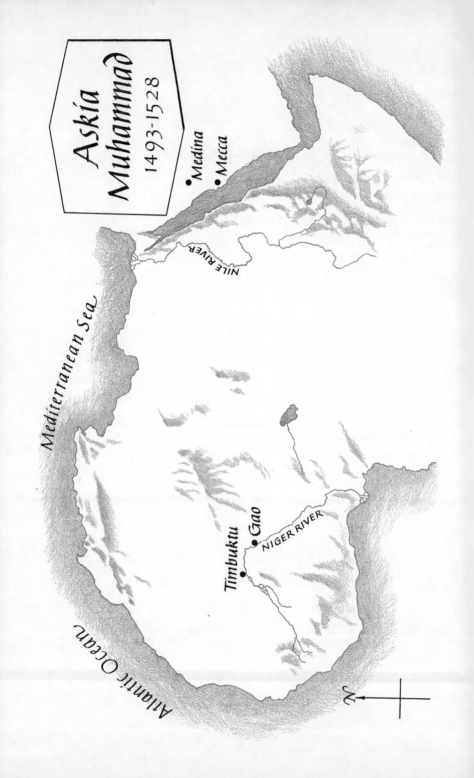

Askía Muhammad
1493-1528

• Medina
• Mecca

NILE RIVER

Mediterranean Sea

Atlantic Ocean

Timbuktu

Gao

NIGER RIVER

The Friday noonday service was over. The Moslem nobles, scholars, and teachers of Gao, capital of the Songhay kingdom, left the mosque. They nodded silently to each other. They were going to the home of one of the scholars to work out a plan to help their country. If the king, *Bakori Da'a* (ba-kor-ree dah), learned of their secret meeting, they would surely be killed or put in prison.

The year was 1492. The Songhay kingdom was in serious trouble. Bakori Da'a had inherited the throne from his father, Sunni Ali Ber. He had been the emperor for only a few months. Already many leaders questioned his ability to rule so large a kingdom.

As soon as the men arrived and sat down on the large silk cushions, their host drew the curtains. He had given strict orders to the servants that he and his friends were not to be disturbed.

The host spoke to the learned group. "If Bakori Da'a stays on the throne, we shall all die."

"Yes," replied a scholar. "He will surely persecute us just as his father persecuted the doctors of the law and scholars in Timbuktu."

A tall scholarly man spoke. "Have you forgotten the tradition of our country?" he asked.

The others waited eagerly to hear what this wise man had to say.

The Moslem leaders of Gao met to work out a plan to help
their country.

"At the beginning of every century," the scholar went on, "God sends a learned man to our people to renew their faith. This is the beginning of the Moslem century. Let us think. Has God sent us such a man?"

"Our ruler must be one who knows what is right. He must have the strength to forbid actions that are wrong. He must be one who can judge wisely and justly between men."

"Bakori Da'a has none of these qualities," the host stated, "but we all know the man who has them. He is Askia Muhammad, head of Gao's armies. He has already proved that he is an experienced leader. He can make the Songhay country strong."

"He is a faithful Moslem," added another man. "He is of royal birth, a noble person. I know his family well. Yes, Askia Muhammad would be an excellent ruler."

"We must first remove Bakori Da'a," said the host. "Then we can have a learned man who has the loyalty and respect of the people as our king."

"Bakori Da'a has reigned less than four months," another reminded him. "The sooner we can remove him from the throne, the safer all our people will be."

A Moslem teacher shook his head. "You cannot overlook the fact that Bakori Da'a has rightfully inherited the throne." This man spoke for the first time. They all saw he was disturbed. "Our emperor is Ali Ber's son. Ali Ber was a Moslem, but he also worshiped the old gods. Naturally, Ali Ber influenced his son. We object to Bakori Da'a because he does not believe as we do. Instead of deposing him, it would be better to try to show him the truth. Let us show him he will be a better king if he will become a true Moslem."

No one said anything for a few moments. They knew they had heard the truth. They argued for a while, but finally agreed. The teacher's plan was good.

"Let's ask Askia Muhammad, whom we trust and admire, to try to convince the king to become a true Moslem."

When Askia Muhammad was told of the plan, he immediately got in touch with a wise Moslem teacher.

"My good friend," Muhammad said, "we have an important mission for you." Then Muhammad told him about the need to persuade the emperor to act like a true Moslem.

The teacher realized the danger of this mission, but he accepted. He traveled to Bakori Da'a's village and spoke earnestly to the ruler.

Bakori Da'a refused to become a better Moslem.

The teacher returned to Gao to report his failure.

"We can't give up this quickly," Askia Muhammad said calmly. "This is too important to all our people. We'll try again."

So the Askia sent a respected scholar to reason with the king.

When the scholar tried to persuade the king, Bakori Da'a became furious. He spoke to the scholar much more sternly than he had to the teacher.

"Go back to him who sent you," Bakori Da'a ordered. "If a third messenger comes to me, let the blood of that messenger fall on your head! Tell Askia Muhammad to prepare for battle. I do not accept his propositions and I never will accept them." His eyes blazed with anger.

The scholar hurried back to the Askia to tell him what Bakori Da'a had said.

Askia Muhammad called his council together. The nobles and scholars were greatly disturbed by the ruler's answer. They also realized that their lives were in grave danger. Nevertheless, they decided that Askia Muhammad should send a third messenger to talk to the emperor.

Askia Muhammad had great admiration for one particularly fine scholar and historian. He chose him for the almost impossible assignment. "Be diplomatic," the Askia told him. "We still hope the emperor will reconsider."

"Go back to him who sent you!" Bakori Da'a ordered the scholar.

The trip was useless. The emperor was angrier than before. He called his army together and had the drums beat loudly as he shouted his refusal to be a better Moslem.

56

Askia Muhammad and his allies pray to Mecca for success in their attack on Bakori Da'a.

"We have no choice then," Askia Muhammad said resolutely when he heard of this. "We will assemble the troops. We will fight Bakori Da'a."

Early in 1493 Askia Muhammad and a small army attacked Bakori Da'a. They were driven off by the ruler's larger army. After the soldiers and their horses had a chance to rest, the Askia led his loyal followers into battle again. The fighting was violent and bloody. This time Askia Muhammad was victorious. Bakori Da'a was defeated. He fled southward to a small village and was never heard from again.

Askia Muhammad then became the king of the Songhay people. In the confusion after Sunni Ali's death and this revolution, many town and village governors had been killed or had fled their posts. The Askia replaced these governors with new people of his own choice. Some were his relatives, who had proved they could be trusted. Others were friends with troops at their disposal.

Askia Muhammad placed his brother in charge of the most important province on the left bank of the Niger. He appointed a number of people to work with him. The important positions included chief of the navy, chief tax collector, chief of forests, and chief of fishermen.

To strengthen the Moslem religion among his people, Askia Muhammad appointed a Moslem judge to every large district. Moslem justice replaced the justice of the traditional law. The Askia's own court became the supreme court of the land, hearing appeals from the lower courts.

Many difficult problems remained from the reign of Sunni Ali Ber. He had been unjust to his people, and the Askia was determined that he would not be guilty of this. There was also pressure on him to reward his followers who claimed they had been robbed by Sunni Ali.

The Askia received sensible advice from a wise counselor. "Do not be driven by your sense of justice to give away all of the state wealth and property left by Sunni Ali."

There was much to be done, also, to make trade routes safe for foreign merchants. After Ali Ber's death, petty chiefs and bandits had begun to raid the traders' caravans. Askia Muhammad was aware of the importance of contact with countries to the north.

The learned men, who had fled from Timbuktu when Sunni Ali captured that city, returned. Askia Muhammad showed that he respected them. To all of them he distributed gold. He consulted them about many problems and gave them special honors.

And he restored Ammar, now an old man, as the Governor of Timbuktu. Since Ammar fled from his "rescuer," Sunni Ali, he had suffered much.

In every way possible, by his own actions and by his practice of the Moslem religion, the Askia tried to show his people the values of being a Moslem. Many did become his followers.

Askia Muhammad had great consideration for his people. He was always aware of their needs. For instance, instead of demanding excessive tax payments, as Sunni Ali had done, Askia Muhammad tried to be fair. Each year at harvest time, Muhammad sent men from his court to receive the crops. If someone was able to give only ten measures of flour, Askia Muhammad's representative accepted that. If others could give twenty or thirty measures, that was accepted. But they were never asked to give more than thirty measures, no matter how much more they might have been able to give. This method was used for all the tribes and occupations.

Askia Muhammad longed to make the pilgrimage to Mecca. As a devout Moslem, he knew it was his duty.

His trusted counselor urged him to go. "Not many African kings have been to Mecca. All your subjects will rejoice that their king has made his pilgrimage. Think how Africa benefited by Mansa Musa's trip."

"A pilgrimage would probably increase trade," Muhammad said thoughtfully. "But I would have to be away five hundred days or more."

"Your empire is in good hands," replied his adviser. "You now have qualified governors and counselors. The affairs of state seem to be running smoothly. Your brother will serve well in your absence."

In 1495, two years after coming to the throne, Askia Muhammad started his trip to Mecca, a distance of about three thousand miles. Even though the Askia's journey was arranged even more elaborately then that of Mansa Musa more than 150 years before, this pilgrimage did not attract the same attention in the Middle East.

But Askia Muhammad's caravan was impressive. There were at least five hundred horsemen and about a thousand foot soldiers. Hundreds of camels car-

In 1495 Askia Muhammad journeyed to Mecca with a great caravan.

ried supplies. Askia Muhammad brought with him 300,000 pieces of gold from the treasure left by Sunni Ali. One-third was to be given away in the holy cities of Mecca and Medina. One-third was for the upkeep of the caravan, and a final third was for the purchase of fine articles in the countries they would be visiting.

Special honor was given Askia Muhammad while he was on this journey. In Cairo he discussed some of his country's problems with several Moslem scholars. The head of the Moslem religion in Egypt made Askia his religious lieutenant in the Songhay country. Askia Muhammad received this honor and the turban that went with it in a special ceremony.

The roll of drums sounded throughout Gao when Askia Muhammad returned in 1497. He was strength-

During his long trip to Mecca, it was Askia Muhammad's custom to distribute dates as signs of his favor.

ened in faith and grateful to come home safely. "Now," he thought, "there is so much more I want to do for my people. We must build a stronger kingdom. We must have better organization. We must add more land and people. And more people should become Moslems."

Muhammad concentrated on extending the borders of Songhay. He kept the professional army Sunni Ali had set up. He enlarged it with captive soldiers and slaves. He divided the army into a number of units. Some soldiers served as his bodyguards. The rest were stationed in other parts of the kingdom under the command of the various governors.

Because the Askia also regarded himself as the leader of all Moslems in the Sudan, he soon began a holy war to convert the pagans. He began this holy war against the Mossi people who lived south of Songhay. The Mossi were the warriors who had taken Walata during Sunni Ali's reign.

He attacked the Mossi and was victorious. He took many children captive. He raised them as Moslems and they later became some of his best soldiers.

During his long reign, Askia Muhammad undertook many military campaigns. Some were planned to keep the nomads under control. Others were begun to capture the major towns and cities along the trade routes. In the west he took two cities from the Mali empire. The ruler of Mali had tried to get help from the Portuguese to stop these attacks, which Sunni Ali began and Askia Muhammad continued.

Later Askia Muhammad took Katsina in northern Nigeria. After that he moved northeast, taking more cities and villages until he had a clear road to Egypt.

Because his army was so strong and well-trained, the Askia was successful in his military campaigns. During his reign, many people accepted the Moslem religion, but he was deeply disappointed that he could not spread the religion farther into Africa. Many people remained pagans.

Askia Muhammad lived a very long time.

His son, Musa, was a collector of taxes. He was an impatient man. He became the leader of a group of men who were jealous of the people close to the emperor, his counselors and friends. Musa made up his mind to take over the throne.

By this time Askia Muhammad was old and blind. His closest friend tried to conceal the Askia's blindness. Musa and his followers drove this friend into exile. The old man was in despair, but the cruel Musa did not care.

In 1528, three of the Askia's sons and his nephew, *Muhammad Mar* (moo-ham-med mar) led a revolt against him. These traitors defeated the army that was sent against them.

Askia Muhammad was forced to give the throne

Old Askia Muhammad despaired at the exile of his friend, but his cruel son did not care.

to his disloyal son, Musa. The old king was allowed to live in the palace, but he had no power or authority. Then, in 1531, Askia Muhammad's nephew, Muhammad Mar, became the ruler.

Muhammad Mar immediately sent his uncle into exile on an island in the Niger River. It was a miserable life, with flies and frogs all around. Askia Muhammad suffered much. He was finally freed in 1537 when another son of his came to power. He was brought back to Gao. He lived only a year more. He died on March 2, 1538, at the age of ninety-seven.

Askia Muhammad's son, Daoud, ruled from 1549 to 1582. The state reached its height at that time. Commerce, trade, and agriculture flourished. The nearby states surrendered to Daoud, extending his kingdom even further. This great power lasted only a few years, however. In 1591, the Moroccans invaded Songhay with guns and destroyed the main part of the empire.

The ambition of Askia Muhammad to convert the entire Sudan to the Moslem religion was not realized when he died. But he did see the expansion of his state. Most important of all, during his reign, he continued the tradition of Sudanese contact with the rest of the world, especially the Middle East and North Africa. Songhay became the Sudanese center of Moslem activities and was a great civilization in West Africa.

AFFONSO I
Christian King in a Pagan Land
(1506–1545)

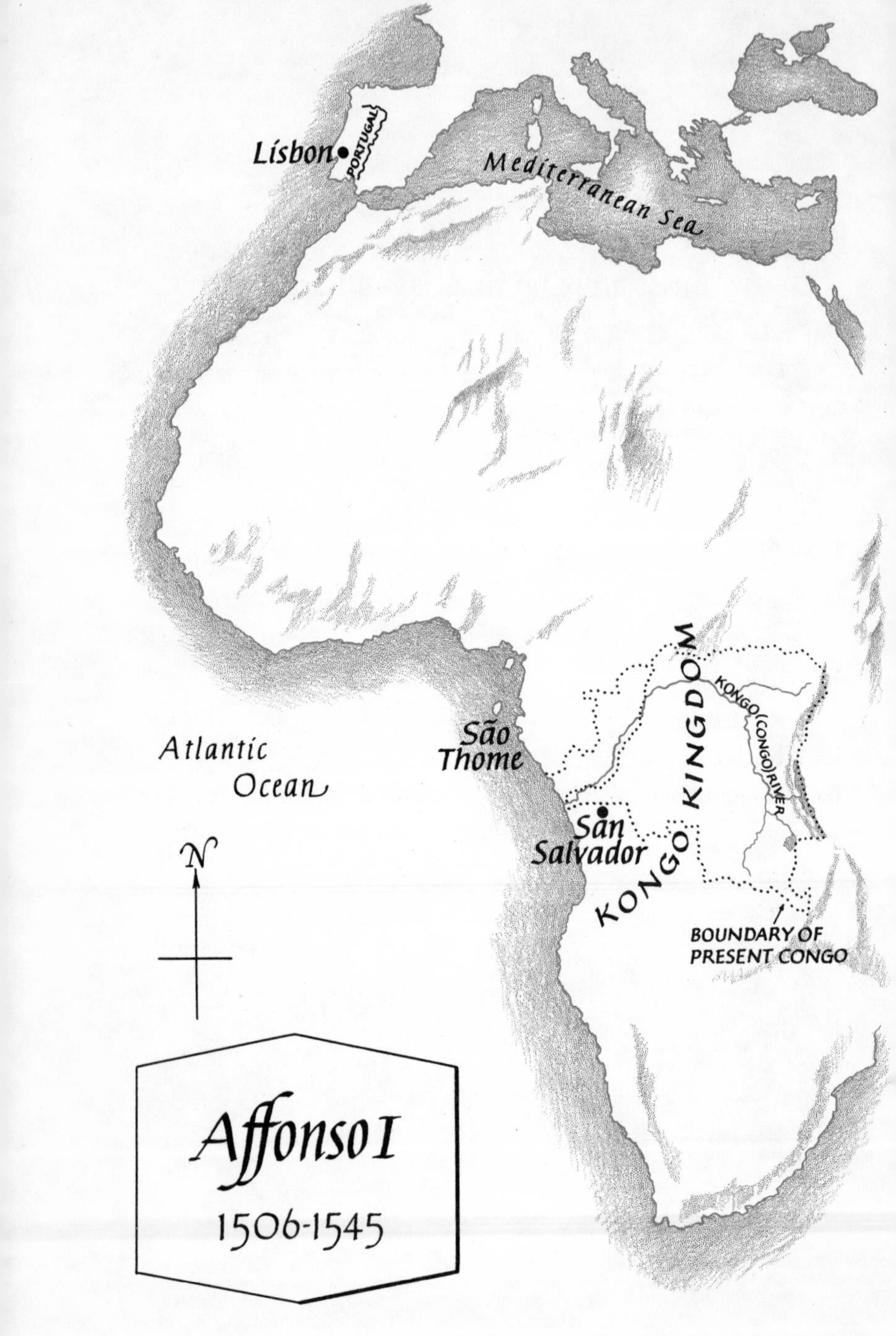

Lisbon •

PORTUGAL

Mediterranean Sea

Atlantic Ocean

São Thome

San Salvador

KONGO KINGDOM

KONGO (CONGO) RIVER

BOUNDARY OF PRESENT CONGO

N

Affonso I

1506-1545

The young prince of the Kongo heard that some strange giant whales had been sighted off the Atlantic coast. He was impatient to learn more about them. Perhaps his father would know.

"How big are the whales? Are they black like a starless night?" he asked his father, who was the ruler of the Kongo.

"They may not be whales," the king answered.

"Then what are they?" the prince asked curiously.

"I do not know. I have not seen them," his father replied. "My son," he said, "I fear these strange monsters will greatly change our lives." It proved to be a prophecy.

The prince left the court, puzzled. He continued to wonder about the mystery of the floating animals in the ocean. It was not until several years later, in 1485, that the Portuguese came inland to the Kongo capital. Then he learned the truth.

The black objects were not whales at all, but small sailing vessels. King John II of Portugal had sent ships to explore the unknown continent south of Europe.

These explorers were searching for a water route around Africa so they could go more easily from Europe to Asia. They also hoped to find the legendary

The Portuguese ships were unlike anything the Kongolese had ever seen before.

Prester John, who Europeans thought was a Christian king living somewhere on the unknown continent. The Portuguese wanted to find a direct route to the markets in Asia where they could buy spices and silk and other valuable things. Then they would not be forced to buy from the Moslem merchants along the Mediterranean. And the Portuguese traders could make more money.

Four men from these ships went to search for the chief who lived inland. They took with them gifts and messages. Their arrival at the court caused great excitement.

The young prince was fascinated by the strange looking men with heavy black beards. The ruler received the Portuguese sailors at his court. But he was suspicious of these people whose skin was so much fairer than his own. They were polite, however, and bowed low to him to show respect. This meeting was important because it was one of the first contacts between Europe and black central Africa. At that time, Kongo was probably the greatest kingdom in that area.

When the foreigners asked in Portuguese, "What is the name of your country?" the king and his son could not understand the language.

The Portuguese explorers smiled. They presented the gifts brought from their far country. They also tried to explain by sign language that they wanted to be friends with the Kongolese.

The strangers from Europe made the king understand that both would benefit if the Portuguese and the Kongolese worked together and if the ruler would accept their religion, Christianity.

The king made them understand that he would like them to remain as his guests. The men accepted the king's invitation.

The Portuguese visitors in the Kongo observed the life of the Kongolese people. They were fascinated by the way these people farmed the land that surrounded their villages. They tilled their soil with crude hoes. When they needed more land to grow more crops, they would slash the tall grass and then burn it. This is known as the slash-and-burn method.

The people were proud of their crops, and carefully cultivated certain grains, such as cereal and forage grasses, and many vegetables.

To their amazement, the Portuguese found that on the edge of the forests the Kongolese grew a strange plant that had been brought from Asia. This gave them hope that they would find a water passage to India.

The foreigners were impressed, too, with the way these industrious people grew palm trees and used the leaves and fruit in so many different ways. They also raised chickens, goats, and some sheep. Hunting was a very honorable activity, but the hunters did not often bring in much meat. Fishermen were also important in communities on all of the rivers and major lakes.

The village houses were built around a central square. The rectangular huts with high pointed roofs were covered with grass and leaves. The walls were made from palm leaves, grass, or wood and dried mud.

The Kongolese made clothes from tree bark or palm leaves. This was in contrast to the Sudanese who grew and used cotton for their garments.

The Portuguese found that the people were skilled in wood carving. The metal smiths of the villages made beautiful jewelry and articles for their huts from iron and copper.

Each village was independent, headed by the eldest man of the local ruling family. Often a small village was composed of people who were all related and a few others who claimed they were relatives, but who might have run away from another village. If the village chief was too strong, that community often broke up when he died because no successor could equal him.

Political organization varied greatly. The smallest political units were the tiny villages under a self-appointed strong headman. Next came groups of villages joined together under a chieftain of one noble clan. Finally there was the great kingdom of the Kongo.

When the Portuguese captain returned from exploring the coast line south of the Congo River, he learned that his men were still at the king's court. He was not certain whether they were alive and well, so he took as prisoners four Africans who had come to see the strange ships with sails that were anchored near the shore. Shortly afterward the captain sailed back to Lisbon, Portugal, taking with him the four Kongolese. Because King John II was anxious to find out about the kingdom of Prester John, the four Africans were royally treated. The Portuguese king hoped to work out a plan with the help of the Kongolese ruler to find this legendary kingdom. While at court, the four Africans learned a little of the Portuguese language and much about the Christian faith.

It was a triumphant occasion when the four Africans returned to their native country months later. They brought many rich gifts for their king. They told him about the strange new foods they had eaten and about the rich clothes worn by the Portuguese.

The prince was impressed.

"What did you do in Portugal?" the prince asked.

He almost wished that he could have gone to the country beyond the ocean.

"We went many times to a big building made of stone," one of the Africans told the prince. "They call it a cathedral. Inside was a gold altar with lighted candles and the priest burned incense." He paused. "This priest sometimes wore a long white robe. Other times he wore a black one. But the Catholic priest is not like our priests that we have here in the Kongo."

"What did the people do in that big building?" the prince asked, more interested than before.

"The people prayed to God, and to His son Jesus Christ. They knelt on the floor and crossed themselves." He made the sign of the cross. "That is the symbol of Christians," he said.

"Do they keep a fire burning all the time in their capital for their king?" the prince asked.

"I did not see it," the African answered. The men told their king all they had learned about Christianity.

"There are many things I like about the Christian religion," the prince said thoughtfully.

The Moslem religion had not come to the Kongo. The people believed in local African religions. They believed in a Creator or High God who was far from the world. There were many less important gods who had powers over disease or rain or other daily events.

The Kongo peoples also worshiped their ancestors. The people feared witchcraft and believed that some objects held magic powers. They worshiped by prayer, sacrifice, and offerings from the first harvest of crops.

It was believed that chiefs and kings had some magic power. It was also believed that an abundance of food and children depended on the king's influence on the gods. The Kongo people kept a sacred fire always lighted in the capital during the life of a king and put it out at his death. The king was the head of the religion.

He was also the very center and heart of the state. As the ruler, he commanded great military strength. He had a personal bodyguard made up mostly of foreign soldiers, who may have been slaves. All the men were called to fight in case of war. They fought battles by forming one huge group and rushing at the enemy. The first clash usually determined the battle. Wars were always brief, because the armies had to go home to tend crops. Casualties, therefore, were light.

The king and lesser officials kept their courts crowded with soldiers, pages, musicians, and servants. They supported themselves by taxing the people in palm cloth (a form of wealth), ivory, animal hides, copper, and slaves. There were tolls on bridges, rafts, pontoons, and a tax on slaves and markets.

There were also court fines, and the king had control of the currency.

At the yearly tax-paying ceremony before the king's palace in the capital, local officials learned if he was pleased with their work. When he was not pleased, they were immediately dismissed.

Between 1485 and 1491, the kings of Portugal and Kongo exchanged ambassadors.

The Kongo ruler asked Portugal to send missionaries, carpenters, and masons. Some were sent. The Europeans promised to build a church and a school in the Kongo. The prince and his friends were interested in the way the carpenters used nails and hammers. They had never seen the kind of saws used to cut the big trees.

It took the Portuguese a long time to persuade the king that some young Kongolese men of noble birth should be sent to Portugal to be trained.

"It is too far away," the king insisted. "We may never see them again."

When he understood the advantages these boys would have, and the help they could give their people when they returned, the king at last agreed.

It was arranged that the king would also send large quantities of palm cloth and ivory on the ships that would sail north across the Atlantic Ocean to Portugal.

Ivory in the Kongo as well as in other areas of

At the yearly tax-paying ceremony, the local officials bow
down before the king.

Africa symbolized royalty. Evidently the strangers did not have much ivory. This was one article the king could use for trade.

The foreigners continued to tell the Kongolese about Christ and His teachings. The king and his son were impressed with the stories of this kindly man who performed miracles. There was something appealing and new about this religion the Portuguese talked about so much.

So, in 1491 the king, his family, and most of the nobility became Christians. The king was baptized with the Christian name John. The prince was baptized Affonso.

The Portuguese continued to ask questions about the Congo River. "How far can you go up the river?" they asked.

"A long ways," they answered. Much of the Congo River is navigable, but the Kongolese did not know how far.

"Is it a big river?"

"Yes." They were sure of that. "It is a river that swallows all others."

This answer was encouraging. The Portuguese hoped that somewhere in Africa they would find Prester John, and so fulfill their king's command.

The king of Kongo was now a Christian, but not a good one. He continued to practice the traditional

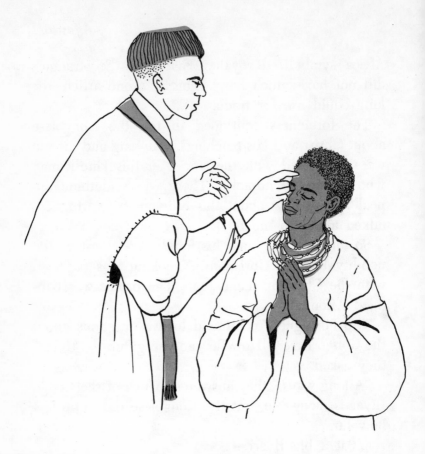

The prince was baptized Affonso.

religion. His son took his new religion as a Catholic much more seriously.

Affonso heard one of the advisers accuse his father of not really believing in Christianity. The prince was deeply hurt. He wanted to defend his father. Instead, he went immediately to the church to pray that his father would come to be influenced only by the teachings the Christians believed in.

But John I, king of the Kongo, had no deep belief in Christianity. Between 1494 and 1506, there was little contact between Portugal and the Kongo. The king and one of his sons gave up the Christian faith then and went back to the religion of their ancestors.

Affonso tried to reason with his father. "You have been baptized. You have chosen this new religion."

The king looked troubled. "Son," he said, "I have many problems. Being a Christian creates many more. I may be the king of the Kongo, but chiefs of the villages, the districts and the provinces also have a great deal of power. They resent our being Catholics." He paused. "This new religion does not mean as much to me as it does to you. I am getting old and cannot fight and argue with the chiefs."

The prince was disturbed by his father's words. "This new faith gives us dignity and strength. When more people believe the Christian religion, we will become a stronger kingdom."

"Affonso," his father interrupted him, "I want you also to give up Christianity."

Affonso was deeply hurt. He said, "Father, I cannot. Being a Catholic has given me strength. I know I can become a finer and better man."

"You must give up the Catholic faith," the king repeated.

The prince refused. Affonso sorrowfully left the court.

Only Affonso and his mother remained Christians.

The king not only gave up the Catholic faith, but he turned against his son. He expelled him to a northern province near Stanley Pool.

A small group went into exile with Affonso. A number of the missionaries went too. After a short time he had an army and he acquired arms. He was also able to persuade some of the local chiefs to accept Christianity. They admired this fine man who was so deeply religious.

King John died in 1506.

A messenger ran through the forest to report to the prince. For even though Affonso and his father had disagreed on religion, the king had recommended that Affonso be chosen king.

Affonso realized that his brother was in the capital. The brother had influence with the electoral council. He hesitated to act.

"If the Kongo is to be Christianized, now is the time," a devout missionary said. "Affonso, if you believe in your religion, and believe that your people can have better lives, then you will have to fight for your rights."

Affonso agreed. "We will fight in the name of God and the Kongo!" he said.

They immediately began to prepare for battle. One evening in late July, on the eve of the Feast of St. James the Great, Affonso and a small well-trained force, including the missionaries, managed to slip into the capital.

During the battle, one of the powerful members of the electoral council, saw a cross high above him in the clear blue sky. He was shaken. Later, people said that St. James the Great and a host of heavenly knights fought for Affonso. Whatever really happened, Affonso won.

Probably the victory was due to superior tactics and discipline which the Portuguese missionaries had taught Affonso's men. Both sides used bows, arrows, spears, and shields. Affonso had conquered the people who did not believe in the Christian religion.

Affonso had his brother executed, but he spared the head of the electoral council. This move helped Affonso maintain a balance between his desire to convert the people to Christianity, and the many powerful forces which opposed him.

Affonso I officially became king of the Kongo in 1506.

He knew he would need help from Portugal to bring about the changes and improvements he wanted for his people. He worried because few of his people were Catholics. Affonso knew he needed many more missionaries. His people should also be trained in more skills, such as carpentry and masonry. So he talked to one of the priests.

"Father," King Affonso said, "I have a favor to ask of you. Will you write a letter to Portugal asking the king to send many priests and technicians to help my people?"

The priest did so. This same priest had encouraged King Affonso to send his son, Dom Henrique, to Lisbon to be educated. King Affonso had resisted this plan for some time.

"Who could be a better example to your people than your son?" the priest reasoned with the king. "He will be trained by Catholic scholars and will attend services in the cathedral. He will have the finest education any prince could have. He may also be sent to Italy to work with the Pope at the Vatican. When he returns to his own country, he will have a message of truth to give to his people."

In payment for the priests and technicians that King Affonso hoped to get, he gave instructions for the ship returning to Portugal to be loaded with copper and slaves.

At the same time, Affonso asked the governor of the Portuguese island of *São Thome* (say-o tow-may) in the Gulf of Guinea to lend him some Portuguese soldiers to help protect his country.

Now began the treachery which was to hurt Kongo-Portuguese relations. The ship's captain kept Affonso's presents for himself. Later, King Affonso asked for cannon, muskets, more missionaries, and even the loan of a ship to transport goods and slaves between Portugal and Kongo. King Affonso did not receive any of these things, even when his personal messengers tried to go to Portugal. Selfish sea captains at São Thome prevented many of his messages from reaching Portugal.

Some slight contact was finally re-established between the two countries. Portugal was especially eager to get some of the mineral wealth in the Kongo. They also wanted to continue the slave trade.

In 1508, an expedition arrived from Portugal with a few technicians and missionaries. From that time on, there were yearly expeditions from Lisbon. And each year Affonso requested teachers, priests, masons, and military technicians. He sent more and more young Kongolese to Portugal for training.

Traders and artisans came from São Thome to help the king. But they were not immune to tropical diseases and almost half of them died within six

King Affonso discussed trade with the Portuguese visitors.

months of their arrival. Those who survived the diseases did not like the living conditions. Then they decided they were too noble to work. They kept their lives quite separate from the Kongolese. This made for bad feelings all around.

Finally Affonso requested that the King of Portugal send someone who could control the two unruly Portuguese groups, the slave traders and artisans from São Thome, and the priests and technicians from Portugal.

Affonso had also asked for legal and military aid. The king sent him the book of Portuguese laws. The ambassador was to act as military adviser. The ambassador and Affonso were to search for "bad" Portuguese and expel them from the land.

In return, the king of Portugal told his ambassador to seek payment in slaves, ivory and copper. The king wanted all trade between Kongo and Portugal to be under his control only. The king also secretly instructed his ambassador to gather all information he could about Kongo.

Affonso rejected most of the advice from the Portuguese ambassador. Affonso found Portuguese laws harsher than the Kongolese law. So he continued to use his own laws. However, he followed the suggestions about schooling, technical training, and missionary work.

He was deeply distressed by the call for slaves in payment. Household slavery existed in Kongo. But selling people into slavery was never done. Affonso did not approve of the cruel slave business. But Portugal insisted and King Affonso had to allow the trade; otherwise the Portuguese aid would stop. He tried to control the trade as much as possible.

Affonso also recognized that his people would not accept many changes quickly. They had to be prepared slowly for new ways. Many missionaries and teachers would be needed to help.

The plan failed completely. It failed because it was not well organized. The local Portuguese were greedy and ambitious. The missionaries and technicians were few in comparison to the slave traders. And many Europeans who did come to help died from malaria, or other diseases.

At first Portugal was willing to help Kongo as an equal. But Portugal also wanted economic gain for itself. The Kongolese recognized this. The Portuguese in the Kongo capital were divided into two groups that were always disagreeing. Some were supporters of São Thome who wanted their island to continue to control Kongo trade. Others supported the king of Portugal. They hoped for rewards in Kongo or at home.

The king was troubled constantly by the skilled

people sent from Portugal. The technicians were always too few and generally refused to work. There were plots, and even murders. There were always too few priests, and practically none would live outside the capital city. Some did not lead good Christian lives.

By 1515 the slave trade had increased a great deal. The technicians and missionaries in the capital insisted upon payment in slaves, as did Portugal. By 1526, the slave trade was completely out of Affonso's control.

In desperation, he wrote to Portugal:

"There are many traders in all corners of the country. They bring ruin to the country. Every day people are enslaved and kidnaped, even nobles, even members of the king's own family."

All these problems frightened the people. They began to think Affonso could not protect them. Some of the chiefs who had become rich from trading with the Portuguese, openly disobeyed the king. Affonso tried to expel all Portuguese traders. He failed, but he did stop their travels throughout the kingdom. He especially opposed kidnaping. Still, by 1530, four to five thousand slaves were exported yearly.

Affonso had once included some silver among gifts and payment sent to Portugal. These, together with the gifts of copper, convinced the Portuguese that there were rich mines hidden somewhere in the Kongo. They sent experts to search. Affonso sent them back before they started exploring.

Actually, the king knew there was only copper in the Kongo, not gold or silver. But Affonso feared that discovery of even these few copper mines would cause the Europeans to invade his country. He refused to tell the Portuguese anything. This only confirmed the suspicions of those Portuguese already in the Kongo.

Away from the capital, the Portuguese would stop a man or woman who was working in the fields. "Where are the gold mines?" they would ask.

They would go to a lonely hut in the forest to ask, "Where are the silver mines?"

To another Kongolese, they would say, "Where are the copper mines?"

In loyalty to their king, the Kongolese would shrug their shoulders and answer, "We do not know."

Portugal stopped other European countries from trading with Kongo. Affonso's pleas for ships or ship builders to aid his contacts with Europe were ignored. The Portuguese did not want Affonso to be able to trade without their help.

In the capital the education program had produced some African scribes fluent in Portuguese. But little more resulted from it. The missionaries and teachers refused to go to the provinces. And, because of the expense, only a few nobles and princes could be sent to Portugal for their education.

Affonso's son, Dom Henrique, was the most outstanding of the youths trained abroad. As bishop, he worked hard to build churches and schools throughout the Kongo. Unfortunately he fell ill, and died in 1526. At that time there were only four priests in Kongo. Most of the Christians were in the capital.

Some Portuguese began to ally themselves with various men who wanted to succeed Affonso as king. This was a dangerous new threat to Affonso. The violent activities of the Portuguese grew so terrible that in 1540, eight of them tried to assassinate the king in church on Easter Sunday. He escaped but had difficulty preventing his loyal people from killing all the Portuguese in Kongo. He died some time between 1541 and 1545, deeply disappointed that his long efforts to educate and convert his people had failed.

Affonso's impact on Kongo was great. His is the only Kongo monarch of the sixteenth century whose history is told in local stories today. He must have been a very clever king. Only such a wise man could have won the throne and faced so many dangers without destroying his country. It seems that he understood the selfish reasons for Portuguese exploration of his land. But he encouraged contact with Europe while doing as much as he could to control the Portuguese traders in the Kongo. Affonso saw the benefits his kingdom could gain from adding the best parts of European culture and skills to its own culture.

IDRIS ALAOMA
Bold Warrior of Bornu
(1580–1617)

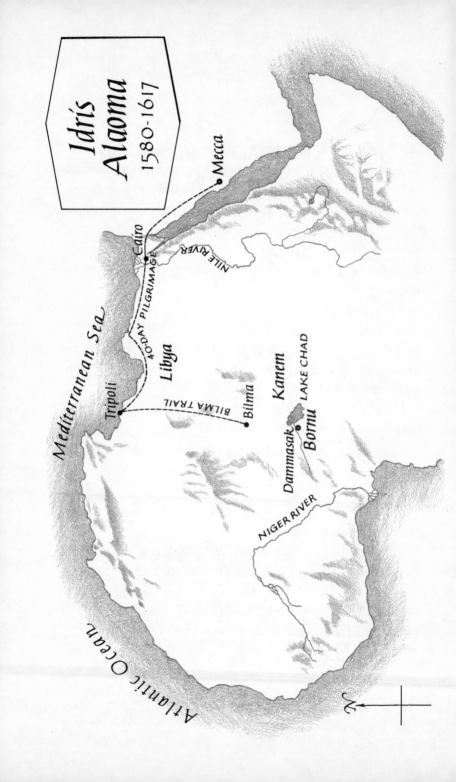

Idris Alaoma 1580-1617

Mecca

Cairo

NILE RIVER

Mediterranean Sea

40-DAY PILGRIMAGE

Libya

Tripoli

BILMA TRAIL

Bilma

Kanem

LAKE CHAD

Dammasak

Bornu

NIGER RIVER

Atlantic Ocean

The boy watched from a small window in the palace. Through the iron bars he could see soldiers with shields and bows and arrows hurry down the narrow street. Anger was written on *Idris'* (ee-drees) dark, brooding face. He should be fighting, too, to protect his country *Bornu* (boar-noo). The bold nomads from the north were terrorizing his people. They had already suffered from many raids.

The soldiers were trying desperately to fortify the village against the next attack. Idris was too young to be in the army. He had even been forbidden to leave the palace. He did not know there was a plot against his life.

Shortly after dark on a moonless night, Idris was taken from the palace. He was heavily disguised. His mother wanted to protect him from the invaders. She secretly sent him to *Kanem* (kah-nem). There he lived with his grandfather among the Bulala people, old enemies of Bornu. Idris stayed there for a number of years.

When Idris' father died, the kingdom of Bornu had been growing in strength and power. The boy was too young to rule, so his cousin had taken the throne. Then the cousin's son had ruled after his father, but he died without an heir.

Idris' mother wanted to protect him from the invaders' plot against his life.

In 1580, Idris, now a strong and wise young man, claimed the throne.

As the new sultan, Idris expected his reign to be filled with warfare. During his childhood, he had become used to raids and sieges. Toward most of the independent clans and villages, he was stern. However, he felt kindly toward the Bulala people because he had grown up in Kanem.

When he announced to his council that he intended to make peace with the Bulala, some of the more ambitious members were upset. But they did not dare to disagree. Idris was able to work out a friendly agreement about the borders of the two states.

"Why do you avoid war?" one of his councilors finally dared ask.

"Why fight if we can be friends?" Idris asked in reply. "This does not mean I will not attack other villages if the need arises," he quickly added. "I intend to make Bornu strong."

The Bornu kingdom of which Idris was sultan had its origins in the Kanem kingdom. That kingdom began in the eighth century, about the same time the kingdom of Ghana was developing between the Niger River and Senegal to the west. But in the western region, Ghana was followed by the kingdoms of Mali and then Songhay. In the Lake Chad area there were only two kingdoms, Kanem and then

Bornu. The dynasty to which Idris belonged was one of the longest-lasting royal families in the history of the whole world.

The early kingdom was located east of Lake Chad. Its people are believed to have been converted to the Moslem religion by Egyptians who traded with them. The state was influenced by Egypt and North Africa. It began to gain power in the first half of the thirteenth century, extending its influence north to *Kauwar* (kow-war) and *Tibesti* (tee-bes-tee), as well as southward. These conquests were made to protect trade routes from raiding nomads.

Then, a century later, a long civil war began between the ruling family of Kanem and their cousins, the nomadic people of Bulala. The Kanem family was driven out of Kanem around 1400 A.D. They then settled on the west side of Lake Chad. By 1507, Idris' grandfather had managed to gain control over both the Kanem people and the Bulala.

It appears that the early people of Kanem were descended from Negro farmers living to the east of Lake Chad and some desert nomads. These white nomads from the north conquered the southern farmers, married into their royal clan, and began speaking their language.

Soon two kingdoms developed. Kanem was on the east of Lake Chad. Bornu was on the west side of the lake.

Bornu had trade contacts with Libya and may even have had trade with Persia (Iran).

Bornu developed and dominated the two routes to North Africa—the forty-day road to the desert Nile and the *Bilma* (bill-muh) Trail north to Libya along the string of oases in the Libyan Desert. Because these routes were safe for caravans, all the city states to the east and west of Bornu sent their goods through Bornu. Thus, Bornu became a greater center of trade than Kanem. Bornu became a meeting place for Libyan and Sudanese commerce and culture. As had happened in other cases, this made it possible for the kingdom of Bornu to become stronger than its neighbors.

In Bornu, caravans from the Hausa city states in the west brought cotton fabrics, leather goods, and kola nuts. They returned south with salt and minerals, as well as Mediterranean and European manufactured goods. They also brought dried fish, ivory, ostrich feathers, and slaves, which were sold to North Africa.

Some of Idris' advisers were troubled when he announced that he was leaving shortly for Mecca. He had received the title of sultan only a little while before this.

When they questioned him, Sultan Idris answered: "I am a Moslem. All true Moslems should go to the holy city of Mecca at least once in their

Much trading took place in Bornu.

lifetime. I have decided it is wiser to go now. I have great plans for Bornu when I return."

While in Mecca, Idris was impressed with the great numbers of Moslems who had journeyed from foreign places to worship and pray. But he was disturbed to hear that many pilgrims had difficulty finding places to stay in Mecca.

"I will build a hotel for Sudanese pilgrims," he announced. "Then more Africans will make this long holy pilgrimage."

And he did.

When Idris made a decision, he did not have to consult his council. He was the absolute ruler of his country. His council of ministers included all of the territorial governors. These men were usually the ruler's favorites or his relatives. They maintained order and collected taxes. They kept a share of the taxes they collected for themselves.

An interesting feature of Bornu was the high rank of some women. The women in Idris' family held important positions in the government. All had their own estates and income, and were active in politics.

On his way back to Bornu from Mecca, Sultan Idris studied the different kinds of weapons used by the states to the north. He was fascinated by the Egyptian army and the muskets which its soldiers used. He had not realized that one weapon could make so much noise.

"If we are to add more lands to Bornu," Idris told his council, "we should have the newest weapons."

His advisers nodded.

"These countries that border on the Mediterranean have much better military equipment than we have. Their soldiers are better trained and better disciplined. Notice, they do not use bows and arrows."

On his trip, Idris had arranged to have some of these soldiers come to Bornu and train his own captains and soldiers. Immediately after his return to Bornu, he began to purchase muskets that were delivered by the traders in the caravans. Sultan Idris also had some Turkish musketeers come to Bornu to train his slave bodyguard. The musketeers proved to be effective against the pagan tribes to the south. The southern people had never seen muskets before.

Idris also maintained corps of shield carriers and archers. When he fought against Kanem, he had a camel corps fight alongside his horse cavalry.

These new methods greatly strengthened Idris' armies. They used the military strategy of sudden, swift marches and so could take the enemy by surprise. When his armies had completed their yearly campaigns, Idris left guerrilla forces behind. These would continue to weaken the enemy until the next big attack.

Idris showed great courage in battle and great

Egyptian musketeers trained Idris' soldiers in the use of the new weapons.

generosity in victory. This impressed his countrymen and others. During his reign many people came to Bornu to live because of his reputation.

His most famous battle was against the *Ngafata* (un-ga-fa-ta). From a heavily fortified town of *Dammasak* (dam-ma-sock) and a few surrounding villages, the Ngafata set out to loot and burn. Idris decided to undermine their power. When they were weakened, then he would begin a direct attack.

He had a camp of fortified walls built near Dammasak. He commanded all the military chiefs to hide arms nearby. Then he ordered them to attack the Ngafata whenever they tried to come outside their walls to harvest crops or pasture their livestock.

He also gave orders to the warriors to cut down the trees surrounding the towns and villages. This would make it even more difficult for the Ngafata to go out unseen.

While the soldiers were cutting down the forests, the Ngafata shot at them with poisoned arrows. The soldiers stopped working and ran for cover.

When his men reported this to Idris, the sultan said, "I have seen those arrows. I am not surprised. They are daring and are good fighters, but we are better."

Then Idris put a wall of shield carriers in front of his soldiers and had horsemen in armor follow. The

Ngafata arrows could then do no harm. At harvest season, Idris' troops harvested the crops and drove the Ngafata away. Subjected to his harsh campaign, most of the Ngafata surrendered and the rest fled far away.

Many, many short campaigns had to be fought all around Lake Chad before Idris was able to restore peace and security to his kingdom. This peace, of course, helped to promote commerce and trade.

From his capital, the great Idris now had time to think about the southern peoples. As a wise ruler, and one determined to enlarge his empire with more land and people, he always kept in mind the importance of trade. Furthermore, some of the tribes to the south were pagans. They had refused to accept the Moslem religion.

He had no trouble in conquering some of the southern tribes. Since they were good soldiers, he added many of their men to his armies. The people of the south were forced to pay Idris a yearly tax.

One of the greatest challenges in the south was the fortified village of *Amsaka* (am-sa-ka) on the black clay plain. For more than a century this village had attracted adventurers and outcasts from the nearby clans. The people of Amsaka were known as the *Yedseram* (yed-ser-am). They considered their village an outlaw haven, free from any authority.

Idris assembled his soldiers and rode against the Yedseram in a surprise attack. To his own surprise, he was beaten back. "We were too anxious and head-strong," he decided. "We will have to prepare our next attack with greater care."

Several years later, when he was ready to under-take a second siege, Idris discovered that the people of Amsaka had cut a deep ditch around their walled city. He gave orders to fill up this ditch. His soldiers went to the fields nearby to gather stalks of grain to put into the ditch.

But when Idris' soldiers withdrew at night, the Amsakans would come out and take the stalks out of the big ditch. This went on for two or three days.

Then one day after the soldiers filled the ditch, again using stalks, other warriors immediately tried to cross the ditch and get to the walled village. The Amsakans, who were guarding the wall, threw flam-ing torches into the wheat stalks.

Idris then built platforms on three sides of the walls so his musketeers could mount the high bar-riers and fire into the village. Again his soldiers filled the big ditch, but this time they used dirt instead of stalks.

"The Amsakans cannot hold out much longer," Idris shouted to his men. "We'll beat our drums loud and strong. The men with muskets will be ready to shoot and close enough to hit their marks."

The noise that followed was terrifying. Battles were usually accompanied by shouting and yelling, but the sound of muskets shooting again and again frightened the enemy. The Amsakans fled in the night, but most of them were captured and executed. From miles around, the people came quickly to surrender to Idris. They agreed to pay taxes to the sultan of Bornu.

Year after year there were peoples to subdue if peace and order were to prevail. While Idris would be busy in the west, a tribe in the south would take advantage of this and raid some of his Bornu villages. The most dangerous enemies were the nomads of the north. Idris sent whole armies and armed columns against the nomads. He himself led three expeditions against them. Peace and increased trade were his objectives. This would make his empire stronger than ever.

The greatest challenge and prize was Kanem. Idris turned to this project with special interest. This was his ancestral home, where the Bulala had been independent for fifty years since his grandfather's day. By taking Kanem, Idris would be reunifying the old empire of Bornu that had flourished in the past.

The Bulala of Kanem now had a new ruler who was unfriendly to Idris. The emperor of Bornu was disturbed. He longed for peace, not war, with the Bulala. But war it would have to be. It took a fierce

Idris was in the front lines in the fight against the Bulala.

attack, with Idris himself fighting in the front lines, to overcome the Bulala army.

Now the victorious Idris could choose the ruler who would keep peace. His cousin, Muhammad, was chosen. Bulala people and Arabs, all residents of

Kanem, were forced to swear loyalty to Muhammad. Some of these people were so impressed by Idris that they followed him home to Bornu to settle.

As did many warriors, Idris died in battle.

Idris was a man of imposing appearance. He was devoutly religious and made his pilgrimage to Mecca. He erected a hotel for Sudanese pilgrims there. He built the first mosque in Bornu to be made of bricks. He worked to replace traditional law with the laws of the Moslem religion. He placed religious judges around him. He yielded to their opinions and submitted cases to them. Because of this, many nobles became Moslems and the people had the benefit of Moslem law. After his second expedition to Kanem, he freed the war prisoners because it had been a political struggle, not a religious war. He always tried to halt wars between two groups of Moslems.

Idris built well. The borders of the empire he established lasted until the nineteenth century, although Bornu had reached the height of its territorial power at his death.

Afterword

There was one goal that was particularly important in the lives of Mansa Musa, Askia Muhammad, Idris Alaoma, and Affonso I. Each of these rulers looked beyond his own kingdom to North Africa, to the Middle East, and to Europe. They all wanted to learn about and use the inventions and knowledge of these other regions for the benefit of their own kingdoms.

For example, Mansa Musa brought an architect and merchants from Egypt and the Middle East. He sent an ambassador to Morocco. He encouraged foreign merchants and traders to come to his kingdom.

The kingdom of Askia Muhammad had been unified by force. He brought Moslem scholars, lawyers and religious leaders to his kingdom from the Sahara and North Africa. He hoped they would help him replace force with one government and one religious faith. The ruler of Egypt appointed Askia Muhammad spiritual leader of all Moslems in Western Sudan. He exchanged letters with leading and religious political authorities in North Africa.

Idris Alaoma, like Mansa Musa, ruled a kingdom which bordered on the frontiers of the Moslem world.

Afterword

To the south of it were unbelievers. He, too, hoped to convert these people to Islam without disturbing vital trade. He brought in Turkish musketeers and colonies of settlers from the Sahara.

All three men saw the need to extend their control over the oases and nomads of the desert. This would assure them supplies of salt and copper. It would protect caravans and lines of trade to North Africa, Egypt, and the Middle East. They also worked to make trade safe inside their kingdoms by firm military control and by unity based on religion and good laws. This would attract merchants, builders, and teachers from the Orient.

Mansa Musa, Askia Muhammad, and Idris Alaoma traveled vast distances to see for themselves what they could try out or import. Affonso did not travel himself but sent his own son and many other young men to Europe for education.

This desire for trade and for the peaceful exchange of knowledge and African goods continues to play a major role in African political, social and economic life to this day.

Sunni Ali Ber, on the other hand, represents the depth and strength of the traditional culture. He was deeply respectful of the old African traditions and religions. Although he was a Moslem, he defended the ancient ways against outsiders, such as the nomads of the north and the Moslem scholars of Timbuktu. Sunni Ali managed to unify in his kingdom many different peoples who spoke many different languages and lived scattered far apart. Often by force but always with respect for local traditions and customs, Sunni Ali made vast lands safe for travel and trade. (However, he aroused the bitter opposition of the devout Moslems in his state. This caused the religious revolution led by Askia Muhammad.)

This search for unity despite different customs and languages is another important goal in Africa today. Now, of course, the idea of African unity is much broader than in this earlier time and includes the whole African continent.

A Guide to Pronunciation

Akil *ah-keel*
Ammar *am-mar*
Amsaka *am-sa-ka*
Arafat *á-ra-fat*
Bakori Da'a *ba-kor-ree dah*
Bandiagara *ban-dee-ah-gah-rah*
Bilma *bill-muh*
Bornu *boar-noo*
Dammasak *dam-ma-sock*
Es-Saheli *es-sa-he-li*
Fagbine (Lake) *fag-bee-nay*
Gao *ga-ow*
Hombori *hahm-boar-ee*
Idris *ee-drees*
imam *ee-mam*
Jenne *jen*
Kaaba *kah-ba*
Kanem *kah-nem*
Kauwar *kow-war*
Mandingo *man-din-go*
Muhammad Mar *moo-ham-med mar*
Ngafata *un-ga-fa-ta*

Niani *ni-ah-ni*
Safa *sah-fa*
São Thome *say-o tow-may*
Senegal *say-nay-gal*
Songhay *song-gay*
Sundiata *sun-di-ah-ta*
Sunni Ali Ber *soon-ni ah-lee beer*
Tibesti *tee-bes-tee*
Timbuktu *tim-buck-too*
Tombo *tom-bow*
Wangara *wang-ga-rah*
Yatenga *yah-ting-ga*
Yedseram *yed-ser-am*

INDEX

Index

Index